ELVIS PR

A Little Golden Book Biography

By Lisa Rogers

Illustrated by Luke Flowers

🌼 A GOLDEN BOOK • NEW YORK

Text copyright © 2024 by Lisa Rogers
Cover art and interior illustrations copyright © 2024 by Luke Flowers
All rights reserved. Published in the United States by Golden Books, an imprint of
Random House Children's Books, a division of Penguin Random House LLC, 1745 Broadway,
New York, NY 10019. Golden Books, A Golden Book, A Little Golden Book, the G colophon,
and the distinctive gold spine are registered trademarks of Penguin Random House LLC.
rhcbooks.com
Educators and librarians, for a variety of teaching tools, visit us at RHTeachersLibrarians.com
Library of Congress Control Number: 2023945564
ISBN 978-0-593-70828-6 (trade) — ISBN 978-0-593-70829-3 (ebook)
Printed in the United States of America
10 9 8 7 6 5 4

Elvis Aaron Presley was born on January 8, 1935, in East Tupelo, Mississippi, in a two-room house built by his daddy. Elvis's daddy worked as a carpenter and in a paint factory. Elvis's mama had jobs in a clothing factory and laundry.

The Presleys didn't have much, but they treasured their son. Elvis and his mama had an especially close bond. They spoke in their own special language as a way of showing their love for each other.

Every week, Elvis attended the First Assembly of God Church. The tiny church was where his parents met and where his uncles preached. As a toddler, Elvis scooted out of his mama's lap, ran up onto the choir's platform, and tried to sing along. From then on, gospel music had a special place in his heart.

Though he loved music, Elvis was shy and didn't sing much outside of church. But when he was ten years old, his teacher encouraged him to enter a talent contest at the Mississippi-Alabama Fair and Dairy Show in Tupelo.

Elvis sang a song about a boy and his dog. He came in fifth place!

For his eleventh birthday, Elvis asked for a bicycle. His mama thought a guitar would be a better gift. That guitar made Elvis a musician.

He taught himself to play, using a book to learn where to place his fingers on the strings. A neighbor showed him how to combine musical notes into chords.

Elvis, still shy about singing in public, brought his guitar to school every day and strummed it during lunch. Soon he started playing at church. Sometimes he sang along.

On Saturday nights, like folks all across the country, Elvis's parents tuned their radio to the Grand Ole Opry's live broadcast from Nashville, Tennessee. The Opry hosted the best performers in country music.

Someday, Elvis declared, he'd perform on the Opry stage!

When he was a teenager, Elvis and his family moved to Memphis, Tennessee. Elvis heard so many different kinds of music there—rhythm and blues, country and western, gospel, and bluegrass. He loved it all.

The summer after he graduated high school, Elvis sang two songs at a recording studio. He said he wanted to surprise his mama.

Elvis had many jobs to help support his family. He worked on an assembly line, drove a delivery truck, and studied to become an electrician. But he kept on singing.

He went back to the recording studio a year later. This time, Elvis recorded a song called "That's All Right," blending country and blues sounds into something new. The studio owner was impressed and gave the record to a deejay at a Memphis radio station. He agreed to play it on his show the very next evening.

That night, Elvis turned the radio on for his parents and then went out to the movies. He was too nervous to hear himself on the radio.

Elvis's mother couldn't believe it when the deejay announced Elvis's name! And he didn't just play the record once. He played it over and over again. Dozens of listeners called the radio station, wanting to know all about this new singer. In one week, thousands of people ordered Elvis's record. It was a hit!

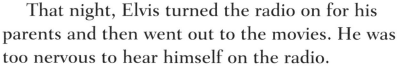

Two months later, Elvis's prediction came true. On October 2, 1954, nineteen-year-old Elvis sang at the Grand Ole Opry!

Soon, it seemed that everyone had an opinion about Elvis. Some people thought his music sounded too different. He also looked different, with his slicked-back hair, pink and black outfits, and flashy dance moves. One TV host refused to have Elvis on his show!

But most people loved his energy, charm, sound, and style. When TV host Ed Sullivan changed his mind and invited Elvis on his show, more than sixty million Americans tuned in. Fans in the audience screamed with delight before he even sang a note of "Hound Dog"!

Elvis rocketed to fame. Some people called his music hillbilly, some called it western bop. One of his songs, "Heartbreak Hotel," became a top hit as a pop, country, *and* rhythm and blues song. The combination of spiritual singing and rhythm and blues came to be called rock and roll. And Elvis was declared the king of this new music.

But Elvis didn't think he was a king. His mama taught him to be kind, respectful, and humble.

Even though he was a big star, Elvis helped people whenever he could. He returned to the Mississippi-Alabama Fair to give a benefit concert. The money raised from ticket sales helped build a park in East Tupelo, where children could swim and play. In New York, he received a vaccine—shown on live TV—to let fans know how they could protect themselves from a disease called polio.

In 1956, Elvis became a movie star, too. *Love Me Tender* was the first of thirty-one movies that he acted in. As soon as Elvis finished a film, he was eager to leave Hollywood and head back home to Memphis. He bought a big house named Graceland and ordered special gates decorated with musical notes.

The inside of the house was just as special. His music room had a white baby grand piano and stained-glass peacocks on the windows. Elvis's den came to be known as the Jungle Room. It had a waterfall and green carpet covering the floor *and* the ceiling!

At Graceland, Elvis rode his golden palomino horse, Rising Sun, surrounded himself with family and friends, and ate his favorite foods—including fried peanut butter and banana sandwiches.

Elvis joined the US Army in 1958 and attended basic training camp in Texas. He could have spent his service performing, or he could have not entered the army at all. But Elvis decided he would serve his country like any other US citizen.

That summer, his mama passed away. Soon after, a brokenhearted Elvis reported for duty in Germany. He brought his daddy and grandma with him to keep him company.

I ♥ MY DaD

   While in Germany, Elvis met Priscilla Ann Beaulieu.
They became close friends. Eight years later, Elvis and
Priscilla got married in Las Vegas, Nevada.
   In 1968, they had a daughter named Lisa Marie.
Elvis adored his little girl and even named one of his
airplanes after her! Elvis and Priscilla divorced when
Lisa Marie was five years old, but he continued to be
a devoted dad. The two had fun at Graceland, riding
horses, playing in the snow, and driving around in
golf carts.

For twenty years, Elvis traveled around the country, performing almost nonstop to millions of fans. In Las Vegas, wearing glittering jumpsuits, he performed twice a day to sellout crowds, singing energetic hits like "Don't Be Cruel" and "Blue Suede Shoes" as well as gospel songs like "How Great Thou Art."

Elvis sold billions of records. He was elected to the Rock and Roll Hall of Fame, the Country Music Hall of Fame, *and* the Gospel Music Hall of Fame.

Elvis died on August 16, 1977, at his beloved Graceland. Each year, more than six hundred thousand people come to honor Elvis and see his home. Graceland was named a National Historic Landmark. Its rooms still look as they did when Elvis lived there.

The boy who was once too shy to sing in public became a legend. Elvis will forever be known as the King of Rock and Roll!